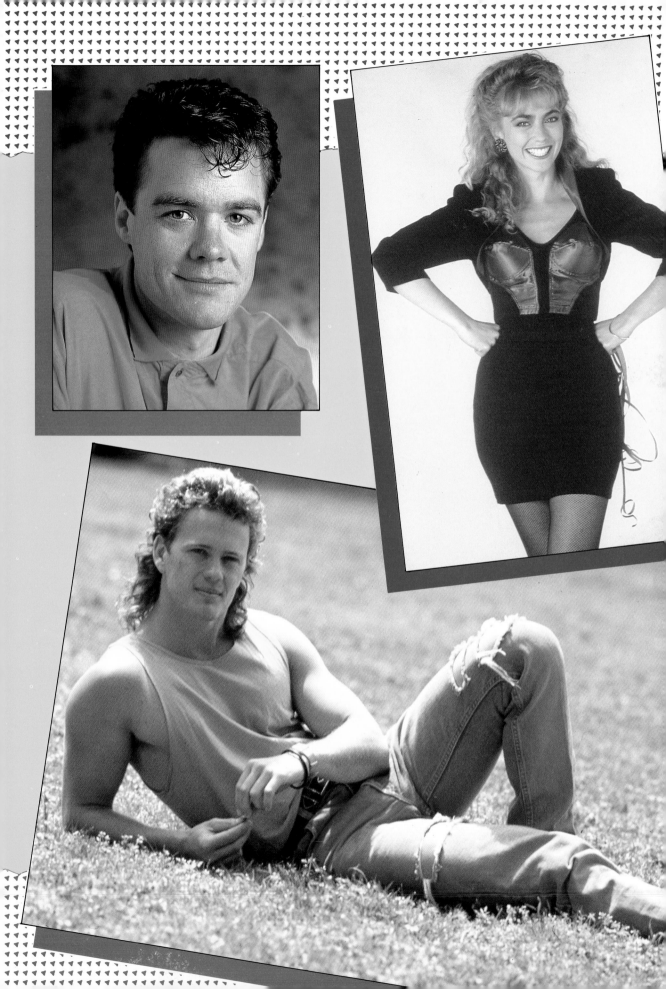

Neighbours™

THE *OFFICIAL* ANNUAL

1991

JOHN McCREADY

NICOLA FURLONG

HAMLYN

CONTENTS

1991

Photographic acknowledgments
All photographs reproduced in this publication were
supplied by Grundy Television Pty Ltd except for
the following:
Topham Picture Library endpapers, 20, 23, 38 top,
39 bottom; Syndication International 4 top right
& bottom, 15, 25, 38 bottom, 39 top.

Published in 1990
by The Hamlyn Publishing Group Limited
a division of The Octopus Publishing Group,
Michelin House, 81 Fulham Road,
London SW3 6RB

ISBN 0 600 57045 2

Printed in Great Britain

'G'day! Welcome to the

*N*eighbours is the television success story of the eighties. A year into the new decade, it seems likely that it will maintain this prestigious position for a long time to come. Nearly every British household has at least one devoted *Neighbours* addict. It's not uncommon for whole families to be glued to the screen for each and every showing of this Australian soap phenomenon. In Britain, where the same episode is shown twice a day, some avid viewers make time for both screenings!

The series began in Australia on 18 March 1985. The ups and downs of life in and around Ramsay Street reached Britain on 27 October 1986. The series was already a resounding success on its home turf. Nobody could have predicted the massive popularity the series has achieved to date. It has made major stars of Kylie Minogue and Jason Donovan who have taken the world's pop charts by storm. Where once British soaps like *Coronation Street* and *Eastenders* topped the television ratings, the friends and families of Erinsborough almost seemed to barge their way to the front of the ratings queue. A side effect of the programme's remarkable success is the fact that the clichéd view of

world of Neighbours...'

Australians as lager-swilling, cork-brimmed, koala-hugging degenerates is now completely out of date. Instead *Neighbours* shows our friends down under as caring, sharing human beings with their fair share of life's joys and dissappointments. In common with the new breed of British soap operas like *Brookside* and *Eastenders*, the characters and events here are as true to life as television ever gets. This is not to say that *Neighbours* doesn't have its fair share of comic moments. Who can forget the antics of accident prone Henry (Craig McLachlan) and devilsome duo Todd and Katie (Kristian Schmid and Sally Jensen) who always seem to end up in another fine mess. To many viewers the inhabitants of Erinsborough seem as familiar as our real neighbours. It's doubtful that you'd mind Paul Robinson (Stefan Dennis) or Jane Harris (Annie Jones) popping next door to borrow a cup of sugar from you. The next best thing is tuning in every day to catch up on the latest adventures of the colourful characters that live on Ramsay Street. Drama! Romance! Comedy! Spray-painted cars called Bertha! Welcome to the wonderful world of *Neighbours*. G'Day!

'Next door is only a foo

Take a stroll down the street where anything can happen, and does . . .

Des and baby Jamie live at the Clarke house, but the door is always open to homeless Neighbours.

tep away...'

There's never a quiet moment with Paul and Gail, the street's empire builders.

Perhaps unlike the neighbours on your own street, some of the people who live on Ramsay Street have been known to move from house to house. With arguments and disagreements rife, these **Neighbours** are always on the move. How many friends do you have that have lived in four different houses on the same street? Bronwyn Davies (Rachel Friend) has done just that.

This street has been the setting for many a barbie, wedding reception and surprise Birthday party. On a more sober note, it has also been the location for fights, accidents and burglaries. Residents come and go, but the fascination of viewers still remains. These wandering Australians are anything but boring!

The interiors of these houses are smart and modern, though some have been accidentally redesigned. For instance the ceiling of Paul and Gail's home which needed extensive repair after Henry (Craig McLachlan) had left the bath water running while looking after the house when the Robinsons were away. Joe Mangel's (Mark Little) makeshift plastering job wasn't quite good enough and hapless Henry found himself with a ceiling on his head!

Henry's love life has led to him moving in and out of Madge's house.

11

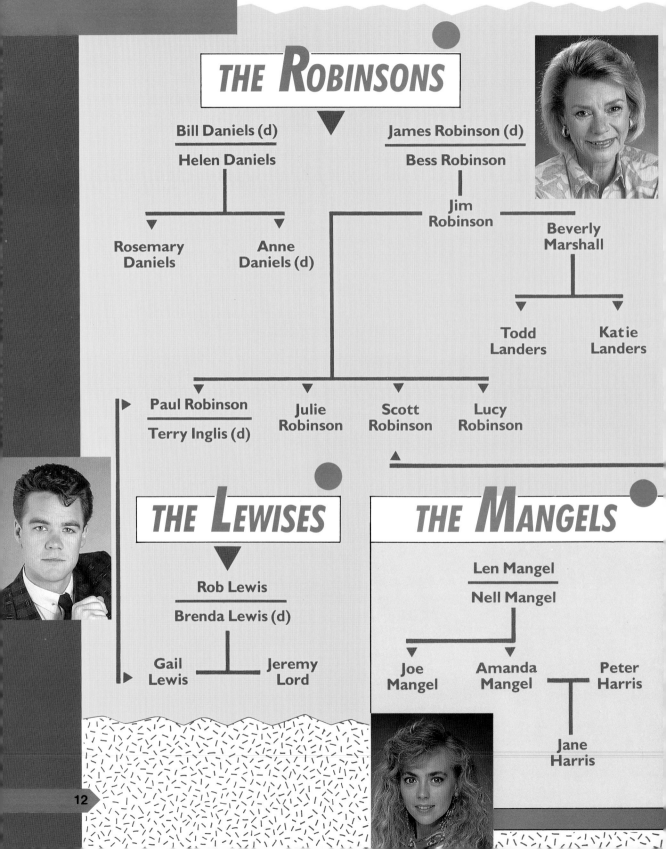

WHO'S WHO

THE ROBINSONS

Bill Daniels (d)
Helen Daniels

James Robinson (d)
Bess Robinson

Rosemary Daniels

Anne Daniels (d)

Jim Robinson

Beverly Marshall

Todd Landers

Katie Landers

Paul Robinson
Terry Inglis (d)

Julie Robinson

Scott Robinson

Lucy Robinson

THE LEWISES

Rob Lewis
Brenda Lewis (d)

Gail Lewis

Jeremy Lord

THE MANGELS

Len Mangel
Nell Mangel

Joe Mangel

Amanda Mangel

Peter Harris

Jane Harris

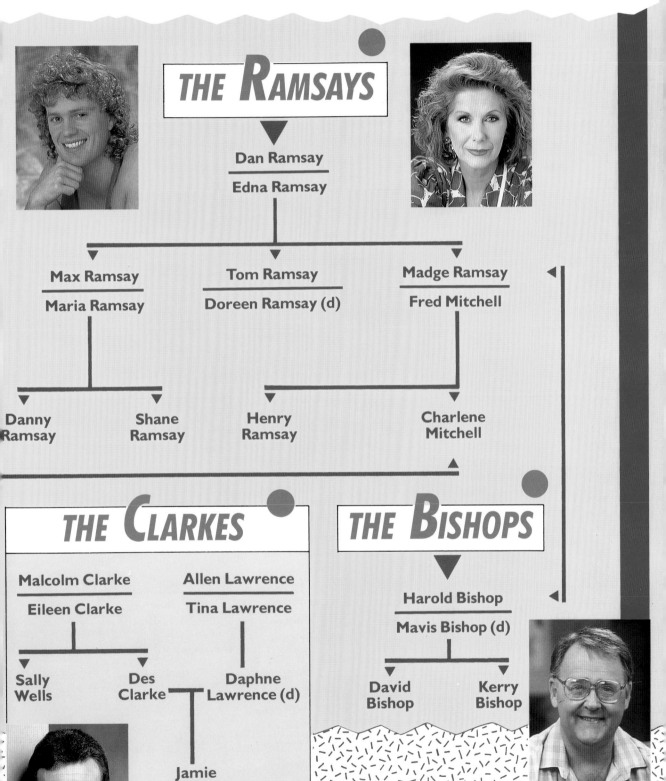

'N RAMSAY STREET

THE RAMSAYS

▼
Dan Ramsay
Edna Ramsay

Max Ramsay
Maria Ramsay

Tom Ramsay
Doreen Ramsay (d)

Madge Ramsay
Fred Mitchell

▼ Danny Ramsay

▼ Shane Ramsay

▼ Henry Ramsay

▼ Charlene Mitchell

THE CLARKES

Malcolm Clarke
Eileen Clarke

Allen Lawrence
Tina Lawrence

▼ Sally Wells

▼ Des Clarke

Daphne Lawrence (d)

Jamie Clarke

THE BISHOPS

▼
Harold Bishop
Mavis Bishop (d)

▼ David Bishop

▼ Kerry Bishop

13

Henry was the Romeo Of Ramsay Street and was content to play the field until Juliet in the form of Bronwyn appeared. After a number of false starts they got together.

RACHEL FRIEND

Bronwyn's first appearance in **Neigh-bours** was an accidental encounter with Des Clarke (Paul Keane) when she mistook him for an uncaring father thinking he had left baby Jamie unattended in a supermarket car park. Little did we know that she would end up as Jamie's full-time nanny and a main character in the series. Bronwyn had moved to the city from the country to escape the pressures she felt after her mother's death. Her father had expected her to take over her mother's responsibilities on the family farm. She was closely followed by sister Sharon who felt she could not live under the iron rule of her father and meddlesome Aunt Edie. To the dismay of the girls, she followed them to Erinsborough and took charge of them again. Strong-willed Bronwyn found she could not take Aunt Edie's interference in her romance with Henry. If Henry ever marries Bronwyn, he will have found a perfect wife as she is obviously maternal yet fun loving. She is the perfect foil for such a madcap personality.

Henry could easily be described as a mad, accident prone fool. Sometimes his tendency to get into trouble can overshadow his true personality – he is a caring man with a heart of gold. Henry hopes one day to be one of Australia's richest men, though it sometimes seems that his money making schemes are hindering rather than helping him achieve his goals. Henry once took to busking, pretending to be a penniless street urchin. He sweet-talked Kerry Bishop (Linda Hartley) into joining him with baby Jamie (S. J. Dey). When Jamie's father Des found out he hit the roof. Henry adds comic lunacy and light-hearted banter to the show. His mother usually defends him knowing that her son never intends to hurt or upset anyone – least of all her long-suffering husband Harold Bishop (Ian Smith).

FARMER'S DAUGHTER

'Neighbours is a drama series not a soap opera. I enjoyed working on it.'

Love makes the world go round and Ramsay Street is no exception. . .

♥

Romance is as much a part of **Neighbours** as it is real life. The Ramsay Street crew do seem to have their fair share of volatile but loving relationships. The most talked about and famous love affair was that of Scott and Charlene Robinson (Jason Donovan and Kylie Minogue). Their teenage romance was the talk of Erinsborough, if not half the world!

Of all the romances in the series no two have ever been alike. Some have ended tragically, like Paul Robinson's (Stefan Dennis) first marriage to Terri Inglis (Maxine Klibingatis), who wounded Paul whilst trying to shoot him. Terri later killed

The nomadic vegetarian and the rough diamond make an incongruous couple

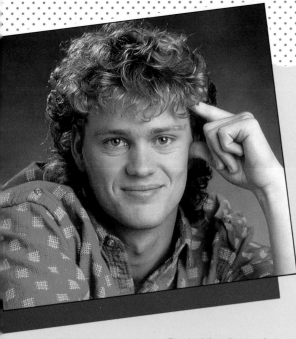

herself whilst in prison. Probably the saddest of all the Ramsay romances was that of Des and Daphne Clarke (Paul Keane and Elaine Smith). The marriage left lovable Des a widower, after Daphne lost her fight for

Des and Daphne Clarke's tragic romance

life when she was injured in a car crash. These love affairs are rarely straightforward boy-meets-girl, boy-marries-girl sagas. No, these liaisons adhere to the rule that true love never runs smooth!

The older couples in the series seemed to have cornered the market in happiness where their love lives are concerned. Harold and Madge Bishop (Ian Smith and Anne Charleston) have a relationship which is summed up by the well worn phrase 'opposites attract'. Harold is a cantankerous and overly moralistic vegetarian who was more set in his ways until marvellous Madge knocked him into shape closely followed by his daughter Kerry (Linda Hartley) who has also had a considerable effect on his attitudes. Madge, meanwhile is very different

'I tried to use myself as a "measure" for Bronwyn'

These blonde bombshells seem made for each other

to her husband. Though she too has high moral standards, she is not so quick to force her views on others. For Madge, Harold is all her philandering first husband Fred (Nick Waters) wasn't. Despite his faults, Harold has been a loving and caring husband since they tied the knot.

Like her father Kerry Bishop (Linda Hartley) has chosen a partner who seems to be so different to her. Joe Mangel (Mark Little) at first seems to be the typical macho man but as his relationship with Kerry develops he becomes more in tune with her broad-minded attitude to life. Joe and Kerry are both parents, and it appears that this factor draws them closer together. It also saved their relationship at one rocky stage, when Kerry's daughter Sky (Miranda Fryer) nearly died after being bitten by a red-backed spider on a day out with her mother and grandfather. They were unable to get help for a few nail biting hours as their car had broken down in the middle of nowhere. When Joe heard what had happened he was first on the scene with comfort for a ▶

'That's when good neighbours become good friends'... and often more than friends!

'I have established so many sides to Kerry. I am sure there are many more . . .'

LINDA HARTLEY

▶ distraught Kerry. His understanding attitude was obviously that of another parent.

Actress Linda Hartley who plays Kerry in the series comments on her character: 'Kerry is nothing like me so it takes a lot of preparation mainly at home to maintain her identity – that's a real challenge'. As for Mark Little who portrays Joe he sees Kerry's love match as having 'a down to earth sense of humour and a quick temper'.

As in most romantic relationships the lovebirds of Erinsborough often find themselves at war with their partners. Scott and Charlene were more often than not at each others throats rather than gazing lovingly into each others eyes! One of their major rifts was caused by a stolen kiss between Scott and Jane Harris (Annie Jones) which almost ruined Charlene and Jane's friendship. Jane herself has had quite a rockly love life. On several occasions she seems to have found the man of her dreams, only to have everything fall down round her ears. Maybe Jane will one day find true love like her grandmother Nell Mangel (Vivean Gray) did when she married John Worthington, and was whisked off to England by her elegant new husband.

However, marriage is still seen as something of value in **Neighbours**. In other soaps it is often viewed as a temporary

Paul Robinson on the trail of Gail

state. The characters in **Neighbours** seem to do everything they can to hold on to their relationships when they appear under threat. Paul Robinson (Stefan Dennis) followed his wife Gail Robinson (Fiona Clarke) to America when she left after he became obsessed with his work.

The relationships of the younger characters are a very important part of **Neighbours**. The love lives of those such as Nick Page (Mark Stevens) and Sharon Davies (Jessica Muschamp) have made the programme perhaps the most popular viewing for teenagers around the world. The fact that the relationships of the younger characters are seen as being as important as the so called adults has much to do with this. **Neighbours** is perhaps unique in the soap genre in that it never patronises its younger viewers. Some of the British soaps could learn a lot from this.

More than swotting was done over the school books when young lovebirds Nick and Sharon were around . . .

Perhaps they could also add to their viewing figures in the process!

Nick and Sharon's relationship is a turbulent one. They play games with each other's emotions. At one point Sharon started to see Nick's arch enemy, Skinner (Matt Stevenson). This caused a great deal of tension as Skinner is a bad sort. As usual they sorted out their differences. Time will tell whether Nick and Sharon's relationship will last. In this programme, things can change so quickly. Only the regular viewers of **Neighbours** can keep track of the are-they-or-aren't-they world of Antipodean romance.

The programme is now so popular that the love lives of the stars are a constant source of media attention. Sometimes the British popular press finds it hard to tell where the fiction ends and fact begins. This has been a particular problem for stars Jason Donovan and Kylie Minogue who have to live their private lives forever shadowed by the prying lenses of Fleet Street.

'GOOD NEIGHBOURS...

Rather more than good friends . . .

Tony Hatch and Jackie Trent are the musical married couple who came up with the distinctive melody that signals the start of the world's best loved soap.

The *Neighbours* theme has been top of the television charts since the programme began. Older readers may also remember that this team of experienced songwriters also came up with the distinctive signature tune that topped and tailed the very popular British soap Crossroads. All together now . . .

'Neighbours . . .'

Grundy Television is an independent television production company, founded 30 years ago, which operates in a large number of countries throughout the world including Australia, the United States and many countries in Europe. Recognised by many people through the success of **Neighbours**, the company also produces such well-known series as Richmond Hill, Young Doctors, Prisoner, Sale of the Century and Going for Gold.

The studios of Grundy Television have grown with the series so that permanent sets like those shown here have been constructed. The way things have been going in terms of viewing figures, **Neighbours** shows no signs of flagging. Such sets are likely to be used for a long time to come!

Grundy Television has built a team which is second to none around the success of the programme.

One only has to look at the end product – the programme itself to see that their standards are exceptionally high. Still the snobs may try to pull the programme down but they can never question its production standards – the equal of any British television production. The viewing figures speak for themselves. In the eyes of the British public, **Neighbours** is the tops! Here's to a successful new decade at Grundy Television, the company that's given us some new Neighbours that have indeed become really good friends!

GOOD FRIENDS'

On the set at Grundy. On TV, they look as cosy as any home. Move back a few yards and the lights and cameras show all isn't quite what it seems . . .

The wonder

Australia – land of many contrasts, where the old meets the new

Far from being the continent of beaches and deserts, Australia has developed into a sophisticated country of many contrasts which in reality is as cosmopolitan, and as advanced, as any of the major nations of the world.

Though still a young country, Australia has made considerable economic advances in recent years. For many Britons the prospect of a job down under is enough to tempt them to this land of opportunity.

Neighbours reflects the new suburban Australia and unveils a new image where cork-brimmed hats and kangaroos seem like ghosts of the long gone past. Melbourne, where the programme is set looks like a scene from an American movie; perhaps a greener New York. The skyscrapers of this prosperous city remind you that this is a relatively young place, a fact reflected in the strong part the younger characters play in the programme.

Melbourne is a good example of Australia as it is today which is why it was chosen as the setting for the series. Though it is set in Melbourne it has been said that **Neighbours** could be about the everyday happenings in any area of the country.

And though it is quite clearly an Australian soap, its appeal has been proved worldwide. Indeed its phenomenal success in Britain perhaps may have something to do with the fact that many British people have relatives in this often green and pleasant Antipo-

Melbourne, a modern city which provides the setting for the adventures of the Ramsay Street regulars

dean land. Whatever, its clear that most of the British that watch it wouldn't give a xxxx for anything else!

So welcome to the new Australia where lager drinking is optional. Only one cliché remains. Yes, the weather is beautiful!

★ ★ ★ ★ ★ ★ ★ ★ ★

Where good neighbours become good friends, and sometimes bad enemies. This is Ramsay Street.

ANNIE JONES
GLAMOUR IS HEP

'Jane's a goody-goody, she's not a bit like me. I get angry and I get mad because I'm a real human being.'

24

SECOND NAME!

Hungarian born Annie Jones now regrets dropping her real name Annika Jasko which is an unusual and memorable moniker. Surprisingly, English (or should we say Australian!), is not Annie's first language, but Hungarian, her native tongue, is.

The character of Jane was originally only meant to be in the series for six weeks, but now Ms Harris is one of **Neighbours** main attractions, especially for male viewers!

Female fans also watch avidly for appearances by the character to pick up fashion and beauty tips from this indisputably attractive member of the cast. **Neighbours** was her first big break.

It comes as no surprise to discover that Annie is a former model, as her natural beauty comes across in every scene. Annie also worked in a number of boutiques and restaurants, in and around Melbourne, before her big break. She jokingly warns us: 'I can mix a pretty mean cocktail'. Her acting career includes appearances in *Sons and Daughters*, the movie *Run Chrissie Run* and a number of pop videos.

It's unlikely that the performers in these pop videos made early on in Annie's career could have known just how high this adopted Australian star would go!

Unlike Jane, Annie has had no problem in finding true love. In the series, Jane has been romantically involved with many handsome men including Scott (Jason Donovan), scandalously after he had married Jane's friend Charlene (Kylie Minogue). Whilst co-stars Jason and Kylie are still footloose and fancy free, Annie has settled down to married life. She tied the knot with boyfriend Paul, a film and TV director who has worked on rival soap *Home and Away*. Now he is married to Annie we are sure Paul will be more often home than away!

Annie Jones has made Jane Harris, Mrs Mangle's granddaughter, very definitely her own. Jane is the bachelor girl of Ramsay Street, but there is never a lack of suitors.

THE YUPPIES

Actress Fiona Corke sees Gail's main appeal to be 'her strength', whilst Stefan Dennis sees Paul as 'unpredictable'. Together they portray the nearest thing Ramsay Street has to yuppies.

STEFAN DENNIS

Unlike his character Paul Robinson, Stefan is not at home in executive suits. He prefers to wear 'mainly jeans or track pants and t-shirts'. Hardly the right kind of gear for the hot shot businessman of Erinsborough. He says some of his favourite actors include Robert de Niro, Meryl Streep, Bette Midler and Dustin Hoffman. He enjoys the comic capers of Jerry Lewis and John Cleese.

Stephen has achieved his status today, he believes through, 'persistence, patience, dedication and believing in myself'. He often feels his good looks hinder him in his chosen career. He told us: 'I wish people would understand that I'm just an actor'. He puts the success of the series down to the fact that, 'it's entertaining and it's about everyday people'.

Fiona Clarke portrays Gail Robinson with a good deal of style and panache. In talking to her we discovered that she was as sharp and as stylish as her **Neighbours** character Gail. She does not have any delusions about her success and she certainly doesn't see herself as an ambassador for Australia. She sees herself rather as: 'An actress in a successful soap who thinks herself pretty lucky to be working'. Of her peers she enjoys the acting talents of Steve Martin, Diane Keaton and Bette Midler. Away from the set, Fiona is happy to spend her time at home, listening to music — reggae, salsa, jazz — or just generally relaxing. She also loves visiting friends and sometimes likes to go to quiet restaurants. Despite this she maintains her trim appearance by using a push bike to get around.

She feels the situations in the programme are 'realistic'. 'It's just that they are compacted down to a group of people in a street, so you can say a lot goes on'. Fiona believes success has made her look into herself a lot more. 'I've discovered and become more aware of the good and bad sides of success.'

OF RAMSAY STREET

'I have no desire
to be a millionaire,
just enough to
live on is fine.'

27

Like work on any television drama series, for **Neighbours**, the production team must work to deadlines with expertise and precision. The programme's production team is made up of some of Australia's finest technicians. For them working on such a successful programme means they have been chosen for their ability to work under pressure, such is the heavy schedule. Unlike some of the best known soap operas, **Neighbours** has established high production standards. Considering it takes many months and millions of dollars to produce a major movie lasting perhaps 90 minutes, it may be surprising that the **Neighbours** team turns out five episodes of quality television per week. That's over two hours of entertainment!

The day on the set often begins before most milkmen have got out of bed! Work starts at around 6.45am. Nobody pretends that it isn't hard work. Many of the stars of the programme have pointed out that **Neighbours** is a particularly demanding job. Three days in each week is set aside for filming. On Monday and Friday, the crucial rehearsals take place. By the time the weekend arrives, the cast and crew are more than ready to enjoy some free time out in the glorious Australian sunshine. Pictures here show the breathtaking location for the Lassiters Hotel complex. ▶

The bridge at the hotel is a beauty spot where many a comic caper has taken place.

SCENES

Welcome to Australia's only six star sunshine hotel . . . LASSITERS

BEHIND THE SCENES

Let's twist again . . .
The Neighbours enjoy
a fifties rock 'n' roll
night at the hotel. Gail
and Madge join the
band at the revival hop

▶ The hotel features heavily in the series. At the Lassiters we are provided with a different view of Australia. In this way **Neighbours** does the job of breaking the belief that this country is all deserts and beaches. The location of the hotel is as green as the English country-side. Our pictures show some of the camera-men from the Grundy production team going through their paces. When you're watching the programme, it's easy to forget that the stars are shadowed constantly by cameras and boom mikes recording their every move.

A day on the set has to run like clockwork if the busy schedule is to be adhered to. By seven in the morning the first scenes, wherever they might be, will have already been recorded. The cast wait in a 'resting room' before going on to the set. Above the studios, the director sits in a dimly lit control room keeping a keen eye on the action. On locations such as those shown in our pictures the temptation might just be to sit back and enjoy the sunshine. Instead the crew is used to working through until dusk. The pictures show some of the hidden faces behind the spectacular success of **Neighbours**. Perhaps these are the real stars of the show!

Getting it right . . .
Whether on the street
or at the beach the
crew are there to get
all the action on tape.

Henry and Nick's day
at the beach isn't as
relaxing as it seems . . .

THE DAD AND

'I call Neighbours a soap and see no shame in that. People who patronise soaps generally don't watch them'

32

THE DOCTOR...

Alan Dale and Shaunna O'Grady have the daunting task of playing model couple Jim Robinson and Beverley Marshall. An exacting job for any actor or actress, yet they seem to cope admirably.

Alan Dale, unlike his character Jim Robinson, is not a widower but a divorcee. He admits now, with hindsight, that he rushed into marriage too young. He married his childhood sweetheart when he was 21 and she was 17. Not something his character Jim Robinson would approve of! Jim is very much a respected man on Ramsay Street who reared four children after the death of his much loved wife Anne during childbirth. He has been helped all the way by Australia's favourite grandmother Helen Daniels (Anne Haddy). Much to everyone's delight Jim found happiness when he married Doctor Beverley Marshall (Shaunna O'Grady). Originally from New Zealand, Alan now lives in Melbourne with his wife Tracey and Terry the poodle. He enjoys the films of Gene Hackman and Meryl Streep.

Shaunna is a coffee-drinking, asparagus-eating Piscean. She appears a little more outrageous than her character Beverley. She lives in three converted train carriages with her lover and her cat. She admires such actors and actresses as Michael Gambon, Julia Blake, Kevin Kline and Tracey Ullman. She is a manic collector with hordes of, 'laces, hat pins, Victorian actress postcards and rouge pots' filling up her railway carriage home. She feels **Neighbours** has helped to change the clichéd view of Australia. 'They know we have suburbs now, not just kangaroos'.

The characters of Jim and Beverley are endearing to viewers as they encounter many realistic problems in their extended family. They are a compassionate couple who have taken in such strays as Beverley's nephew and niece Todd and Katie and the one time lone wolf Nick. Their door is always open for any of their **Neighbours** who may need a shoulder to cry on or a sympathetic ear.

ALAN DALE

Even though Neighbours is seen as a soap it is never short of great drama.

The drama which comes into our homes with **Neighbours** is often nail-biting stuff. It comes in many forms . . . fires, robberies, near fatalities, road traffic accidents, attempts at blackmail, poison pen letters, runaways, missing persons. The list is endless, and it's what keeps us all glued to our television sets. At the end of most episodes there is usually a cliffhanger of an ending, and these normally are of great dramatic content.

Many of the **Neighbours** have come out of these dramatic situations as heroes and heroines. When Des Clarke (Paul Keane) and Joe Mangel (Mark Little) had a

Des and Joe make a bet

bet over conquering their fears, Des came out a rather reluctant hero. He saved Joe's life when the mighty Mangel nearly drowned during Des's part of the bet, which was to overcome his fear of the water. Des was reluctant to become Joe's 'friend for life', as he felt intimidated by his overwhelming friendliness.

Sadly, some of the dramatic episodes which have been featured in the long-running series have ended in death. One of the shows best remembered moments was Daphne Clarke's (Elaine Smith) tear-jerking death-bed scene when she bid a sad farewell to her devoted Des. The happiness which the couple had brought to the show was much missed. Though not everything in the Clarke's garden had always been rosy. They had had their fair share of drama like everyone else in exciting Erinsborough. There were tense moments when baby

A normally madcap Henry captured in a more sombre moment

Jamie Clarke (S. J. Dey) was seriously ill in his first weeks of life.

Poor Jamie nearly found himself an orphan when his father was trapped in the coffee shop during a fire. Luckily, his life was saved by a helping hand from heroes Harold Bishop (Ian Smith) and Paul Robinson (Stefan Dennis).

Blackmail is a nasty word in any circle, and Ramsay Street is no exception. When Helen Daniels (Anne Haddy) was left a seemingly substantial amount of money by Jim's late mother Bess. It was believed at first that Helen had been left $150,000 but it soon came to light that they were Hong Kong dollars, not Australian dollars and therefore only worth about $20,000 in Antipodean currency. The money caused more trouble than it was worth when Helen received blackmail threats demanding $20,000 or the safety of her family would be in jeopardy. Super sleuth Katie (Sally Jensen) discovers that the blackmailer is her father Bob. The drama heightens ▶

As the coffee shop burns, Des is pulled to safety by his friends

Henry keeps watch
from his car hoping to
spot the culprit

'The situations are realistic, it's just that they are compacted down to a few people. A lot happens'

FIONA CORKE

▶ when she and her brother Todd (Kristian Schmid) are torn between loyalty to their father or loyalty to the Robinsons who they love deeply. Todd finally tells the Robinsons but his father is caught by the police anyway. Despite the heartache Bob had caused the Robinsons, they put up his bail and allow him to stay with them for a few days to be with his children.

Blackmail letters are not the only thing that have arrived in the mail to cause drama in Ramsay Street. Bronwyn Davies (Rachel Friend) was the subject of a series of malicious and upsetting poison pen letters. She enlisted the help of her then estranged boyfriend Henry (Craig McLachlan) to help her track down the literary fiend. The drama escalates when Henry, who has held an all night vigil in his trusty wagon Bertha, awakes to witness the culprit getting away on his motorbike. In an attempt to save Bronwyn from further upset over the disturbing contents of the letters, he unsuccessfully tries to hide the new letter from her. She jumps to the wrong conclusion thinking Henry has been sending the nasty correspondence. Her belief that Henry would do such a thing is too much for him to take and it would have seemed that any chance of reconciliation between the two was impossible. When Bronwyn comes to her senses, she realises that affable Henry would never stoop so low. However, her ex-boyfriend it appears would, as it is revealed that he is the real culprit.

Hospitals seem to be one of the main settings for many of the dramatic scenes which have occurred in the series. Helen's

Helen pulls out of a coma

weeks in a coma proved to be a trying and emotionally draining time for her friends and family. The good souls of Ramsay Street set up a rota to keep up the everyday chatter which they hoped would rouse Helen out of her comatose state. Luckily their hard work and dedication paid off.

It was also in the local hospital that Scott (Jason Donovan) was once reunited with Charlene (Kylie Minogue) after she had nearly suffocated in a fire. He realised how much he loved her when he nearly lost her.

But drama is not something that just happens on a grand scale, it can happen within the four walls of a family home. Mike Young (Guy Pearce) found himself involved in a family drama when he was a student teacher. Whilst privately tutoring student Jessie Rose (Michelle Kearley) he discovered that she was being beaten by her

mother Adele Ross (Marian Sinclair). It is ironic that it was Mike who found this out as he himself was once the victim of parental beatings. He is angered when, even after Jessie's father (Doug Bennett) discovers what has been going on, it appears that he is more scared of what could happen to his business reputation if the story gets out, rather than the effect it is having on his daughter. Even though he is only young, Mike has had enough experience to be able to deal with such dramatic incidents in a sensible way.

The excitement and tension which the drama included in **Neighbours** brings is an integral part of its continued popularity. It would seem that the scriptwriters who have the characters lives and futures in their hands are going to keep us all on the edge of our seats for many years to come.

Thankfully, not many of us have as much drama in our lives as the inhabitants of Ramsay Street. Most of us, I'm sure, are happy to simply watch the unfolding dramas played out for us by our cousins down under.

Another dramatic episode in the lives of the Neighbours

The showbiz

For a country with a relatively small population Australia has produced a host of stars . . .

CLIVE JAMES

Apart from the cast of **Neighbours,** of course, Australia is a land where stars seem to pop out of the outback on a daily basis!

Whether it be comedy, drama or the serious world of top journalism and writing, the stars of Oz are more than a match for the best entertainers from around the world.

Like Paul Hogan and Barry Humphries the cream of Australia's showbiz community have made it very big on the international stage and have risen to the very pinnacle of their chosen fields in America and Europe.

In the world of comedy, Australia seems able to produce an endless stream of talented performers. Paul Hogan is perhaps the best known film star the country has ever produced. He hit the big time in the blockbusting *Crocodile Dundee* series of movies which centered on the comic capers of a cobber new to the American way of life. Paul has often been described as Australia's answer to Benny Hill and

ROLF HARRIS

Wizards of Oz

was the star of his own TV series based around similar songs and sketches.

Rolf Harris is one of the country's best loved performers. His style appeals particularly to children. They love his talent for on the spot art and his musical mastery of the wobble board. He has given us all many a laugh. His catch phrase, 'Can you tell what it is yet?' is an everyday expression instantly associated with the bearded humourist.

The numerous bizzare personalities of satirist Barry Humphries are so convincing that many people think he actually is Dame Edna Everage or the famed Australian cultural attaché Sir Les Patterson. These fictional personalities mock the world's often clichéd view of Australia and Australian culture. Sir Les

BARRY HUMPHRIES

PAUL HOGAN

and Dame Edna are so obviously surreal that the clichés become ridiculous and obviously untrue.

Clive James is a true ambassador of his country. A university educated writer and expert commentator on Australian culture, he now lives and works in Britain where his popular TV show takes a comic look at television around the world. Clive is certainly not your average cobber!

> Helen Daniels is a real trouper, despite illness and family problems, she always comes up smiling. It looks as though Katie Landers is following her as a tough cookie.

SALLY JENSEN

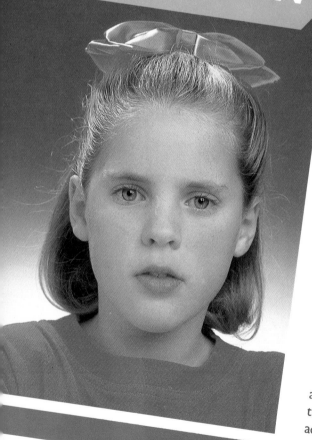

Sally Jensen is a loveable little girl who ha. brought charm and innocence to the show. As Katie she has had quite a tough life and deserves some happiness, which she seems to be getting now she lives in Erinsborough. Sally is enjoying life as one of the **Neighbours** cast. 'I particulary love Craig and Jason' she admits. What little (or big) girl doesn't?

Katie has found a wealth of happiness through the love showered on her by Helen. Anne Haddy who portrays Helen on screen describes her character as 'a great lady'. Anne, like Helen, is a lady of great taste who loves to eat sushi, drink champagne and wear beautiful clothes. She is happily married to actor James Condon who played Douglas Blake in **Neighbours**. She credits him as her favourite actor, with Bette Davies ranking as her favourite actress.

She feels the programme is 'as realistic as a drama can be', and believes it is set, 'anywhere in Australia, not just Melbourne'. She enjoys travelling enormously. 'I loved going back to London recently'. She has always felt emotionally attached to Britain: 'When I play the music of Elgar, I think of Britain and cry'. Like her character, Anne has many friends whom she misses a great deal now she and James have had to move from Sydney to Melbourne because of the demands of the show. She says of **Neighbours**: 'Many people say they don't watch the show, but they do. Some don't like to admit it — that's their problem'.

Anne's main ambition is to: 'Stay alive to enjoy being with my husband, my children, and my grandchildren'. Sentiments Helen would sympathise with.

Young Sally hopes one day to be as good an actress as Anne. She feels since starting work on the show she has learned a great deal about acting.

LEADING LADIES

'By 10 I wanted to be a nurse. By 12 acting was going to be my life'

REBELS WITH OI

'Nick is a street kid and I find playing him very natural. 50 per cent of him is me'

WITHOUT A CAUSE?

Though they do appear rather rebellious at times, the characters Nick Page and Todd Landers are the loveable rogues of Erinsborough. Both have had a rough time in the past, but it seems life in Ramsay Street is helping sort out their young lives for them. Actors Mark Stevens and Kristian Schmid who play Nick and Todd are likeable young men who haven't let fame go to their heads.

Mark lives in Melbourne and feels at home in jeans and T-shirts, writing music, playing golf, practising Kung Fu or even weightlifting! He admires Richard Gere and Michelle Pfeiffer and enjoys the music of Simply Red. His favourite ways of getting about are a Nissan Pulsar Q, and a ten-speed racing bike. Despite his achievements as an actor, Mark is primarily a singer and hopes one day to be able to concentrate more on his songwriting with the aim of becoming, 'a successful international recording artist.' Who knows? Maybe one day he'll follow in the golden footsteps of Jason! Mark's family are very proud of him and he told us: 'They encourage me in all I continue to strive for'.

Kristian Schmid feels, even though he has achieved success at such a young age, it has not spoilt his childhood, which he still enjoys. He likes listening to The Beatles and The Doors, eating Italian food, especially pasta and lasagne. His favourite drink is soda water. His hobbies include water skiing and collecting cigarette lighters.

Kristian reckons the series owes a lot of its considerable success to the fact that: 'It has its own style and makes people feel good', and that 'suburban Australia is reflected in **Neighbours**'. To Kristian, Britain seems: 'Like it is at the other end of the world. But I hope to visit there soon'. Hopefully we will be seeing a lot more of the boys in the future.

When a window has been smashed or there's trouble at Erinsborough High, young rascals Nick and Todd are often blamed. Even when they're not guilty!

KRISTIAN SCHMID

HOW WELL DO YOU KNOV

Put you and your friends to

the test with our special

Ramsay Street Mastermind Quiz

1 Which school do the young Neighbours go to?
2 Who got trapped in the coffee shop fire?
3 Who was fooled by Hong Kong Dollars?
4 Who was wrongly blamed for sending Bronwyn poison pen letters?
5 Which international Australian star plays Crocodile Dundee?
6 Which Australian TV star is also a top journalist in the UK?

7 Can you tell what it is yet? Which Australian comic said that?
8 Who is the man behind Dame Edna Everage?
9 Whose real-life musical tastes include, 'everything but heavy metal'?
10 Whose favourite pop group is Sigue Sigue Sputnik?
11 Who has two dogs called Ebony and Kinny?
12 Who lives with 13 sheep and a turtle?
13 Which rock star did Scott and Mike send their tape to?

14 Who plays baby Jamie Clarke?
15 Who left the bath water running?
16 Who though Des had abandoned his baby in the car park?
17 Who was Paul Robinson's first wife?

18 How did Daphne Clarke die?
19 Who got bitten by a red-backed spider on a day out?
20 Who stole a kiss from Scott and upset Charlene?
21 Who left for England with a new husband?

22 Who is Nick Page's arch enemy?
23 Which star enjoys the comic capers of Jerry Lewis?
24 Name the TV company that produces Neighbours.
25 Which actress lives in three converted train carriages?
26 Which star is married to actor James Condon?
27 The series is set near which Australian city?
28 Whose real life favourites are The Beatles and The Doors?
29 Whose real name is Annika Jasko?

YOUR Neighbours?

30 Which star appeared in the film *Run Chrissie Run*?
31 Who is a subtle and sympathetic Piscean?
32 Which keen writer and vegetarian is a Virgo?
33 Who shares his star sign with Marylin Monroe and Judy Garland?
34 Who wrote the Neighbours theme?
35 Jason or Kylie? who sang 'Never Gonna Give You Up'?
36 Which team produces songs for Jason and Kylie?

37 Who played Scott before Jason Donovan?
38 Who has a stepfather called Reg in the series?
39 Which character used to be an airline stewardess?
40 Where was Alan Dale (Jim Robinson) born?

ACROSS

1   The capital city of Victoria State
3   The Neighbours characters are now super . . . .
5   Jane's uncle's name
8   Where is Mrs Mangel living
10 Who looks after Jamie
12 Paul's father-in-law's name
15 Scott's career
16 What is Harold's daughter's name
17 What's the name of Gail's first husband
19 Who fell off a ladder, trying to get a bird
22 Australian native with thick grey fur
23 Someone from another country
24 Where is Charlene living
25 Good jumper that doesn't wear clothes
26 Wild aussie dog
27 Beverly and Jim's nephew and niece come from where

DOWN

1   What has Mike recently sold
2   Where do our characters live
4   Beverly and Jim's nephew's name is
5   Who did Mike propose to
6   Henry's grandfather's name
7   Nick is known for this illegal form of art
9   Which is the largest city in Australia
11 A small kangaroo-like marsupial
13 Jim's first wife's name

14 Harold who eats no animal food is one of these
18 Scott's mother-in-law's name
20 A native from Australia
21 Beverly and Jim's niece's name

ANSWERS ON PAGE 61

45

The Bishops are two of Neighbours best loved characters. Life is never dull when Madge and Harold are around. Life for Anne Charleston and Ian Smith is much the same. . .

IAN SMITH

From the age of four, when Anne saw her first panto, she knew acting was for her. Whereas Ian admits: 'I first wanted to be a musician'.

Anne is a lady of classic tastes — she loves drinking champagne and eating seafood, with a soft-spot for oysters. Her musical tastes she describes as 'catholic', liking classical, especially Mozart and Vivaldi, as well as some opera, good rock and roll, and musicals. Of her peers in the acting profession she enjoys Vanessa Redgrave, Peggy Ashcroft, Michael Gambon and Ben Kingsley, to name but a few.

Anne is a social butterfly. 'I like going to the theatre, especially to see plays and the ballet. I also like having friends over for long lunches. I have the same friends I've had for years, and I still socialise with them.' When cheekily interrogated as to whether romance plays a part in her busy life, she says, 'I have several men friends, most of them purely social. There is the one occasional one who means more than that.' Whilst out gallavanting, Anne enjoys wearing evening gowns by her favourite designer, Mariana Hardwick.

Whilst Anne enjoys sipping champagne, Ian likes a tot of whisky. He like Harold, 'is capable of every human emotion and can swap and change at a moments notice'. He is happily married to wife Gail, with whom he shares a bungalow in Melbourne.

He too, like Anne, has varied musical tastes, enjoying 'jazz and classical — in fact everything but heavy metal.' Ian likes his chosen profession. 'As an actor, the world is my oyster'. He began on his road to success as a member of a local amateur drama group, admiring the work of Sir John Mills and Glenda Jackson. He dismisses the condescending snobbery of critics of the series. 'Snobs are born with a self image problem. Remove the problem and there would be no snobs.'

ANNE CHARLESTON

STREET'S ODD COUPLE

'There's a bit of me in Madge – but more of my mother, and qualities I have observed in other people'.

47

Feuds

Everybody likes to get on with their neighbours but sometimes things don't run so smoothly. . . .

The Shorter Oxford English Dictionary defines a feud thus: 'A state of bitter and lasting mutual hostility especially such a state existing between two families, tribes or individuals, marked by murderous assaults in revenge for some previous insult'.

Antipodean feuding thankfully hasn't yet led to death but our friends on Ramsay Street can sometimes get a little hot under the collar for many and varied reasons.

Probably the longest lasting feud in the series concerned the name of the street itself. It is still a thorn in the Robinson Family side as they believe the rightful title should be Robinson Street!

Ironically, one of the feuds concerning the younger residents of Ramsay Street was

Love leads to many a feud, which often involves fists!

about making it in the music business. Charlene's (Kylie Minogue) arch rival Sue Parker (Kate Gorman) invented a cruel practical joke to try to get revenge on her rival and also to pay Mike (Guy Pearce) back for preferring Jane (Annie Jones). She concocted her plan after hearing on the Erinsborough High School grapevine that

Superbitch Sue Parker plays a cruel practical joke.

Scott (Jason Donovan) and Mike had composed what they believed to be a smash hit pop record. With this belief they had sent it off to Monk McCallum a successful rock star and producer.

Superbitch Sue duped the boys into believing that she was the star's secretary, and invited them over to his house to perform the number for him.

Feuds often lead to sorting out the macho men from the blundering boys.

Gullible Scott and Mike fell hook line and sinker for the hoax, even making a special demo tape with Charlene on backing vocals. They boasted about what they believed to be their break into the pop world to their

Scott and Mike make Charlene a star

school friends, and before long the whole school knew! Naturally, when they arrived at McCallum's house they were sent away as he had never even heard of them!

Like mother like son, Joe is often in the middle of a fiery feud.

'Sharon doesn't think before she acts which often leads to her getting into trouble.'

JESSICA MUSCHAMP

► True to form, Sue was around to tell the world of their misfortune. But, as always seems to happen in this particularly long-lasting feud, Sue's plan backfired.

Monk McCallum's manager appears as he believes their work has potential, but that the boys should stick to songwriting as the real vocal talent was Charlene's backing vocals! Obviously a man who knows his music. Sue was left infuriated that her plans to belittle the three friends had gone wrong. It ensured that this feud would continue in the series.

Love has been a common denominator in many of the feuds in **Neighbours**. Long time friends Charlene and Jane (Annie Jones) fell into a feudal state when Charlene

Engine trouble . . . Sparks fly over the spark plugs at the garage.

discovered that her 'friend' had been kissing her husband! Joe Mangel's (Mark Little) new found love for Kerry Bishop (Linda Hartley) fuelled the feud that had already been simmering between himself and her father Harold (Ian Smith).

Henry (Craig McLachlan) found himself on the receiving end of a great deal of hostility, and a punch from Mike when he returned from touring with a jazz band. Mike was feeling pretty bad after the tour anyway and, finding on his return that not only had Henry moved into Mike's home but also into his ex-girlfriend Bronwyn's (Rachel Friend) bedroom!

As well as coming between friends and neighbours, feuds can cause rifts in once

Sharon and Bronwyn fall out at the coffee shop

happy families too. The usually loving Davies sisters found themselves feuding after Sharon loses her job at the coffee shop and Bronwyn takes over her apron. Luckily, in the end, the girls realise that blood is thicker than coffee!!

For as long as the series lasts, it looks pretty certain that the Ramsays (be they Bishops or Mitchells, or even Robinsons!?) and the Robinsons will always be feuding over one thing or another, be it street names, trees, sporting feats, their children's marriages or, as is usually the case, not much at all really!

Shaz v Bronny — a feud tugging at the apron strings. . . .

COMIC MARK AND

'I share my house with a cat, two mice called Kylie, two kids and two women.'

TOE-TAPPING LINDA

Actor Mark Little breathes a sigh of relief, I'm very different to Joe, thankfully'. He views himself as an actor and comedian which seems obvious from some of the comic capers he has brought to our screens.

Mark lives in Melbourne in a Victorian weatherboard house — very conventional. However, he displays a bizzare side to his nature in telling us his favourite drink is rainwater, his favourite food is raw fish and his favourite pop group is bizzare Sigue Sigue Sputnik!

Off screen he likes to wear 'Levi's 555s, cowdy boots, and a selection of hopefully interesting but always comfortable upper body coverings'. His ambitions are to travel around Australia and to further his film work. Perhaps he hopes to follow eventually in the footsteps of his favourite actors Jack Nicholson and Robert de Niro.

Home for Linda Hartley is: 'In an extremely multi-cultural, cosmopolitan inner-city suburb in Melbourne'. Her home life is very precious to her: 'I have a wonderfully "large" double-fronted Victorian home which I share with my beautiful husband'.

Linda reckons the series 'depicts Melbourne's "suburbia" very well', and owes its popularity to 'the sun, the friendly atmosphere of suburban Melbourne and colourful characters wearing colourful clothes!'. Kerry being one of the most colourful residents of Ramsay Street, Linda's tastes in clothes include: 'Loose flowing elegant pants and short dresses that show off one's legs'.

It seems possible that Linda could prove a star in other fields too: 'It would be great to make a record as I've been singing and dancing since I was six. I'd really like to keep pursuing musical theatre as well.' It's clear Linda is an extremely talented lady.

Following his mother's fiery footsteps, Joe Mangel burst into the world of Neighbours like a bat out of hell. He's now stepping out with batty Kerry Bishop.

LINDA HARTLEY

STAR SIGNS

PISCES

Linda Hartley. Subtlety, sympathy and tact make up the Piscean personality. Linda is a typical Piscean in that she is good natured and easy going. Throughout her career she has shown a quick understanding and willingness to learn — both Piscean traits. Linda shows she is a true fish as they have vivid imaginations and first rate powers of expression. As an actress she makes good use of these skills. Pisceans frequently follow two or more occupations at the same time, and Linda's parallel interests in drama and music show she could at some point follow both interests. The main fault of those born under this sign is that they often feel unappreciated, something Linda isn't among her many fans.

LIBRA

Fiona Corke. Libra is the sign of pleasure, beauty, elegance and harmony. Librans have the ability to compare things and reach an impartial judgement on them, but at the same time, they dislike argument, often sitting on a fence in a debate. Fiona is typically Libran in the stylish fashions she sports. She has an eye for colour, and likes to look unusual in her dress sense as do many fellow Librans. Many outstanding fashion designers and interior decoriators are born under this sign. It comes as no surprise that as a Libran Fiona entered the world of acting.

VIRGO

Jessica Muschamp. The main trait of Virgoans is their analytical mind. Often, they are mistaken for being reserved and unfeeling. This is mainly because they often want to conceal their contradictory and nervous nature behind a businesslike front. Jessica is typically Virgoan in that she has an excellent eye for detail and is genuinely inventive. Her love of writing and painting is symbolic of those born under this sign. These people are noted for their questioning natures and her decision to become vegetarian is an example of that. They are reliable and make good friends.

GEMINI

Ian Smith. Like fellow Geminians, Marilyn Monroe and Judy Garland, Ian Smith is charming, intellectual and at times restless. Those born under this sign make excellent companions and are entertaining and witty story tellers. Gemini people are usually born with the ability to charm the birds from the trees. Like Ian, most Geminians change their moods to fit their environments which means they seldom lose control of themselves or of situations and are good to have around in an emergency.

CAPRICORN

Anne Charleston. The sign of the Goat symbolises practical, diplomatic, shrewd and economical people. Anne seems to be a typical Capricorn with her clever and subtle intellect, and her ability to be a true friend. Capricornians like to be in charge. They are ambitious and usually achieve great wealth. The negative side of their natures can be seen in their selfishness, something Anne seems to have conquered.

CLARKEY AND

If little S. J. Dey (baby Jamie), grows up anything like his onscreen father, Paul Keane, or his favourite 'uncle' he certainly won't be making a mistake!!

PAUL KEANE

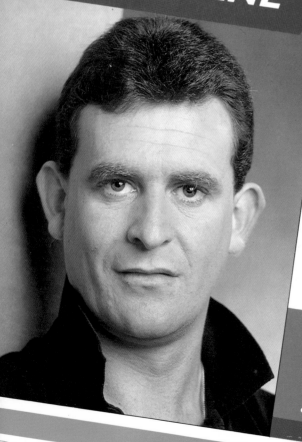

We have Paul Keane's sister to thank for introducing us to her brother, as it was she who encouraged him to join in amateur theatre with her. His closeness to his family is obviously of great importance to him, as is his mum's roast dinner, which he credits as his favourite meal!

Paul couldn't be happier relaxing at home, dressed casually in black jeans, drinking ice cold beer in the company of his girlfriend Ellen, and their dogs Ebony and Kinny.

He is a keen drummer who enjoys Australia's own brand of rock 'n' roll, with Cold Chisel as one of his top bands. He prefers to get around on foot, having lost interest in cars when he was almost killed whilst drag racing!

Like Mike, Guy Pearce has had his seemingly unfair share of bad blows in life. His father died when he was only eight years old and his sister Tracy is mentally handicapped. Despite his tragedies, Guy has always maintained a stiff upper lip. His love for his family is strong and his devotion to his sister is heartwarming.

His portrayal of Mike as a jazz musician is pretty close to home as his real love is the life of a rock 'n' roll musician. 'I've always been interested in music and I've been writing songs for over seven years. You come home after a long wrenching day at the set and it's relaxing to sit for hours at the piano and tinker with different ideas'.

Well Guy can make music with us anytime!

'Everyone involved works hard to make Neighbours as realistic as possible.'

YOUNG MR. MIKE

'The last thing I want to do is show half the world an awful looking body.'

RAMSAY STREET

'I laugh so much at work – we have a great time – like a happy funny family'

Residents Rule O.K.!

Actresses Jessica Muschamp and Anne Scott-Pendlebury have certainly made their mark, and it looks like as if young Ashley Paske is following their rise to the top.

U2 fan Jessica is a stalwart vegetarian who lives with her parents, 'a beautiful dog called Roo, four cats, six horses, some chickens, thirteen sheep, four budgies and a turtle!!!', on a ten acre farm about an hours drive from Melbourne. She loves the peace and tranquillity of the countryside which is something she doesn't exactly get a lot of, especially when Hilary is around! She hopes to be a successful writer as well as an actress, with writing and painting as hobbies.

Jessica sees Erinsborough as neither Melbourne or Sydney, rather as a bit of both. With British Citizenship (her father is British) she cannot wait until the day she gets to work in the UK.

Ashley Paske (as Matt Robinson) is new to the show but is already creating a stir. Will Bronwyn (Rachel Friend) fall for him? or will she stay with Henry (Craig McLachlan)?

ANNE SCOTT-PENDLEBURY

ASHLEY PASKE

FANS...FANS...FANS...

For those who can't

N E W S

RAMSAY STREET

WELCOME TO ISSUE 1

NEW KIDS ON THE STREET

TODD AND KATIE LANDERS – KRISTIAN SCHMID AND SALLY JENSEN – CHARACTERS INTRODUCED EP. 661

Kristian and Sally were originally contracted for thirteen weeks but it has now been extended. They play Beverly and Jim's nephew and niece who come to stay with the

MESSAGE FROM THE EDITOR

Here it is at last. The Official Neighbours Fan Club has taken several months for us to put together the Neighbours Fan Club package for 1990. Between us the Fan Club, the BBC in England and Grundy T.V. Australia we think we have succeeded in putting together a first class package for all of you who have been patiently waiting for an Official Fan Club. We know that many of you have written away to unofficial clubs and have been disappointed which is why everybody concerned with Neighbours agreed that an official Fan Club should be launched.

Further issues of the Ramsay Street News will be sent to members throughout the year at approximately 4 monthly intervals – so watch out for issue No.2. Some of the things to be included in issue No.2 – features of more of your favourite characters and one or two you may not know yet, answers to crossword and word search and an to enter competition.

r's death he the Robinson

t Mark on just keeps tion with now ned the cattered kes est of

Robinson employed him as manager and Tony promised to stay on at least until Charlene's training was finished. After the arrival of Tony's mother and the news that his father was unwell Tony decided to return to Perth.

CHARLENE ROBINSON – KYLIE MINOGUE –CHARACTER INTRODUCED EP. 235

Scott and Charlene were offered a house of their own in Brisbane by Madge's father and after much discussion and heart pulling Charlene has moved to Brisbane to prepare the house for when Scott an join her.

OFFICIAL *Neighbours*

FAN CLUB

et enough of life down under . . .

Neighbours is a series which has inspired total devotion. For some people two showings a day just isn't enough. If you feel that way then the Neighbours official fan club is the ideal solution for you too. As well as providing you with an introductory package of Antipodean memorabilia, they'll keep you informed of what's going on in Erinsborough with the regular Ramsay Street news!

If you wish to join the Neighbours Fan Club please send a stamp-addressed envelope to The Neighbours Fan Club, P.O. Box 136, Watford, Herts WD2 4ND.

NAME *NATALIE FENWICK*

is an official member of the Neighbours Fan Club.

DATE *18TH JUNE 1990*

ADDRESS *12, KING ROAD, ANYTOWN, DEVON*

TQ6 9FB POSTCODE

SIGNATURE *Natalie Fenwick*

Answers to quiz on pages 44 and 45

1 Erinsborough High 2 Des Clarke
3 Helen Daniels 4 Henry 5 Paul Hogan
6 Clive James 7 Rolf Harris
8 Barry Humphries 9 Ian Smith
10 Mark Little 11 Paul Keane
12 Jessica Muschamp 13 Monk McCallum
14 SJ Dey 15 Henry 16 Bronwyn
17 Terri Inglis 18 A car crash
19 Sky, Kerry Bishop's daughter
20 Jane Harris 21 Nell Mangel
22 Skinner 23 Stefan Dennis
24 Grundy Television
25 Shaunna O'Grady 26 Anne Haddy
27 Melbourne 28 Kristian Schmid
29 Annie Jones 30 Annie Jones
31 Linda Hartley 32 Jessica Muschamp
33 Ian Smith 34 Tony Hatch and
Jackie Trent 35 Neither; Rick Astley
36 Stock Aitken Waterman
37 Darius Perkins 38 Paul Robinson
39 Gail Robinson 40 New Zealand

ANSWERS

ACROSS

1 Melbourne 3 Stars 5 Joe 8 England
10 Bronwyn 12 Rob 15 Journalist
16 Kerry 17 Jeremy 19 Hilary 22 Koala
23 Foreigner 24 Brisbane 25 Kangaroo
26 Dingo 27 Adelaide

DOWN

1 Motorbike 2 Erinsborough 4 Todd
5 Jenny 6 Dan 7 Graffiti 9 Sydney
11 Wallaby 13 Anne 14 Vegetarian
18 Madge 20 Aborigine
21 Katie